Photo credits:
Fotostudio Klaus Arras in collaboration
with Katja Briol: P. 4 (above and 2nd from
bottom), 5 (2nd from bottom and bottom),
37, 43, 45, 47, 49, 55, 57, 58, 73, 74, 119,
123, 127, 129, 130, 133, 135
TLC Fotostudio: all the rest

Illustration:
Carmen Strzelecki: P. 7

Cooking for Friends

Contents

Foreword

Dining with friends is one of the most enjoyable ways to spend your free time. Whether getting together for a barbecue on a balmy summer's evening or celebrating an occasion with an elegant dinner, such evenings are likely to remain with you as pleasant memories long after the event. This book contains a comprehensive selection of great recipe ideas which are bound to be a big hit with your guests. We have also included below a few suggestions designed to inspire you with creative ideas for decorating your table and hints on how to arrange your plates, glasses and cutlery correctly. A meal should, after all, be a feast for the eyes as well as the taste buds.

A few creative ideas can be turned to magical effect in just one or two simple steps. Candles are an absolute must when entertaining. They can be used in profusion, instantly creating a festive atmosphere. Tea lights, in particular, are ideal for producing a variety of simple candlelight arrangements: placed in a coloured glass vessel, such as a Moroccan tea glass, they will cast beautiful, coloured reflections over the table. They can also be used to decorate individual place settings. Alternatively, an elegant effect may be achieved by arranging these tiny lights in a line across the table or by simply dotting them romantically around the table.

Flowers, plants or foliage are also key elements in table decoration. Single petals scattered randomly over the table create a capricious, romantic effect whilst an autumn get-together could be celebrated with an arrangement of colourful, freshly gathered foliage and chestnuts. Herbs, with their wonderful Mediterranean scents and aromas, also make a delightful contribution to the dinner table.

Classic rules for setting the table
Each guest should be allocated around 80 cm of table space to be able to sit comfortably. You may wish to provide each place setting with a service plate on which the individual dishes pertaining to each course are placed during the meal. A side plate is placed to the left or above and to the left of the service plate.

Traditionally, knives go to the right of the plate, with the blade edge facing inward. Forks are placed on the left, with the prongs pointing upwards. The cutlery should not lie flush with the lower edge of the plate, but approximately a thumb's width above it. The arrangement of the cutlery reflects the sequence of courses on the menu. Accordingly, the cutlery needed for the starter is placed on the outside whilst the main course cutlery is situated on the inside. The soup spoon should be placed horizontally above the plate, with the dessert cutlery beneath it. The golden rule, therefore, is to start with the cutlery on the outside and, course by course, work your way inwards. The one exception to this is the bread knife, which should be placed across the side plate. The glass intended for use with the main course should be placed more or less above the main course knife. The water glass, which remains in use throughout the meal, should go just to the left of this and any glass to accompany the starter goes on the right.

Gazpacho jelly with olives

Serves 6

8 gelatine leaves
1 slice day-old white bread
4 tbsp olive oil
400 g tomatoes
1 green and 1 red bell
  pepper
300 g cucumber
4 spring onions
2 garlic cloves
2 tbsp sherry vinegar
salt
pepper
ciabatta
green and black olives

Preparation time: 40 minutes
  (plus chilling time)
Per portion approx.
  210 kcal/880 kJ
6 g P, 8 g F, 29 g CH

1 Soften the gelatine in cold water. Cut the crusts off the bread and soak in the olive oil. Wash the tomatoes, remove their stalks, then dice. Wash and dice the peppers. Peel and dice the cucumber. Slice the spring onions into rings. Purée all the ingredients to a smooth paste in a blender along with the peeled garlic cloves and vinegar, then season with salt and pepper.

2 Press the water out of the gelatine and dissolve in a saucepan over a low temperature. Stir the dissolved gelatine into the vegetable purée, then spoon the mixture into the compartments of a clean ice-cube tray and chill in the fridge until set.

3 Divide the ciabatta into slices, top each slice with a gazpacho cube and thread onto skewers with green and black olives.

Stuffed mushrooms
with walnuts

Serves 4

4 sundried tomatoes, in oil

50 walnuts, chopped

115 g cream cheese

salt

pepper

12 medium-sized
  mushrooms, stalks
  removed

50 g Manchego cheese,
  freshly grated

2 tbsp freshly chopped
  coriander

a few iceberg lettuce
  leaves

bay sprigs

olive oil, for greasing

Preparation time: 20 minutes
  (plus grilling time)
Per portion approx.
  229 kcal/961 kJ
8 g P, 21 g F, 12 g CH

1 Drain and chop the tomatoes. Roast the walnuts in a frying pan without fat, then mix the nuts with the tomatoes and cream cheese.

2 Clean the mushrooms and wipe with a damp cloth, then fill with the walnut mixture. Grease a baking tray with oil and arrange the mushrooms on the tray. Grill for approx. 7 minutes under a hot grill. Sprinkle the grated Manchego over the top and grill for a further 5 minutes. Sprinkle with coriander. Using a bay stalk, skewer the mushrooms to a slice of walnut bread topped with an iceberg lettuce leaf.

3 Alternatively, the mushrooms may be stuffed with a mixture of spinach, cream cheese and chopped pine kernels. For this variation, wash, blanch and chop the spinach. Mix with toasted pine kernels and cream cheese, then stuff and cook the mushrooms as described above. Thread the mushrooms onto slices of walnut bread, topped with iceberg lettuce leaves, using sprigs of bay or rosemary.

Cheese appetisers
with olives and capers

Serves 8

150 g cream cheese
  with herbs

8 tbsp olive oil

50 ml milk

salt

pepper

200 g broccoli florets

4 slices of toasted white
  bread, halved

4 black olives

4 spring onions

4 capers

Preparation time: 20 minutes
  (plus cooking and grilling
  time)
Per portion approx.
  210 kcal/880 kJ
5 g P, 18 g F, 8 g CH

1 Beat the cream cheese, oil and milk together until creamy, then season. Wash the broccoli and cook in boiling, salted water. Divide the florets between four halves of toasted bread, top with half the creamy cheese mixture, then bake under a hot grill for approx. 10 minutes until golden brown. Garnish with olives.

2 Wash and cut the spring onions in half, then cook for approx. 10 minutes in a little salted water. Drain and leave to cool. Divide the spring onions between the 4 remaining slices of toast, then top with the rest of the cheese-and-cream mixture. Bake under a hot grill as above, then garnish with capers.

Prawns
with salsa verde

Serves 4

12 large prawns
1 small, red bell pepper
1 spring onion
30 g butter
½ tsp mustard powder
2 tbsp dry sherry
1 tsp Worcester sauce
50 g cooked fish
3 tbsp breadcrumbs, for
   coating
1 tbsp freshly chopped
   parsley
1 tbsp mayonnaise
salt
pepper
1 egg
50 g grated Parmesan
250 ml salsa verde
   (ready-made)
baked garlic bread, sliced
green olives

Preparation time: 30 minutes
   (plus cooking and baking time)
Per portion approx.
   530 kcal/2220 kJ
20 g P, 36 g F, 29 g CH

1 Peel the prawns, leaving the tails intact, then wash and pat dry. Cut along the top of each prawn and open out the body.

2 Wash and dry the bell pepper and spring onion, then finely chop. In a frying pan, sauté the pepper and onion in 15 g hot butter, then add the mustard powder, sherry, Worcester sauce, fish, breadcrumbs and parsley, and continue to cook for a few more minutes.

3 Lightly beat the mayonnaise with the salt, pepper and egg, and combine with the mixture in the pan. Spoon the filling onto the prawns. Melt the remaining butter and drizzle over the prawns. Sprinkle cheese over the top and bake the prawns in an oven pre-heated to 180 °C (Gas Mark 4, fan oven 160 °C) for approx. 10 minutes.

4 Spread the *salsa verde* onto slices of garlic bread. Thread 1 stuffed prawn and a green olive onto each slice of garlic bread.

Squid on white beans

Serves 4

1 garlic clove
2 spring onions
8 tbsp olive oil
300 g fresh squid, ready
  to cook
250 g white beans, cooked
salt
pepper
1 tbsp balsamic vinegar
2 tbsp freshly chopped,
  flat-leaf parsley
2 lemons

Preparation time: 30 minutes
  (plus cooking time)
Per portion approx.
  310 kcal/1300 kJ
18 g P, 21 g F, 13 g CH

1 Peel and chop the garlic clove. Wash the spring onions, then slice into thin rings.

2 Heat 3 tablespoons of olive oil in a frying pan. Wash and dry the squid, then cut into slices. Sauté the squid in the hot oil along with the garlic and spring onions for approx. 2 minutes. Add the beans and cook for 2 minutes. Season with salt, pepper and vinegar, then stir in the parsley.

3 Divide the mixture into small bowls. Cut the lemons into eighths and garnish each portion with a lemon segment on a wooden cocktail stick.

Black pudding pinchos
with sherry

Serves 4

1 onion
2 garlic cloves
2 tbsp oil
1 tsp dried thyme
1 tsp paprika powder
225 g black pudding (or
  Morcilla blood sausage)
2 tbsp dry sherry
½ ciabatta
bay sprigs

Preparation time: 20 minutes
  (plus cooking and frying time)
Per portion approx.
  390 kcal/1630 kJ
14 g P, 25 g F, 26 g CH

1 Peel the onion and garlic. Slice the onion into rings and finely chop the garlic. Heat the oil in a frying pan, then gently fry the onion rings and diced garlic. Add the thyme and paprika powder, and sauté all the ingredients for approx. 5 minutes.

2 Cut the black pudding into 12 slices, add to the frying pan and cook for approx. 3 minutes on each side until crisp. Pour in the sherry and continue to cook until all the liquid has evaporated.

3 Divide the bread into 6 slices, cut each slice in half and spread with the onion-and-garlic mixture. Using a bay sprig as a skewer, thread a slice of black pudding onto each piece of bread.

Lamb snacks
with mint and honey

Serves 4

200 g lamb
½ tsp ground cumin
1 tsp mild paprika powder
salt
pepper
2 tbsp olive oil
8 leaves each of sage
   and mint
150 g boned lamb
1 tsp mustard
2 tbsp honey
12 slices of wholemeal
   baguette

Also:

Aioli for garnishing and
   basting

Preparation time: 30 minutes
Per portion approx.
   400 kcal/1670 kJ
29 g P, 16 g F, 34 g CH

1 Wash the lamb, pat dry, then dice the meat. Combine the spices and oil, cover the meat with this marinade, and leave to rest for approx. 30 minutes.

2 Wash the herbs, then shake dry. Remove the meat from the marinade and thread on a skewer, alternating each piece with sage and mint leaves. Grill the kebabs for approx. 8 minutes, turning frequently and basting with the marinade. Serve with aioli.

3 Wash the boned lamb, pat dry, then cut into 1-cm thick slices. Season with salt and pepper, and brown under a hot grill for approx. 2 minutes.

4 Turn the meat over, spread mustard and honey on the uncooked side and grill this side for a further 3 minutes until crisp. Using a sprig of bay, thread each piece of meat onto a slice of toasted wholemeal baguette topped with a little aioli.

Lomo embuchado
with ratatouille

Serves 4

4 green bell peppers
1 onion
350 g aubergines
300 g courgettes
350 g tomatoes
2 tbsp olive oil
salt
pepper
1 tsp each of freshly
  chopped thyme and
  oregano
200 g lomo embuchado
  (dry-cured ham)
4 sundried tomatoes in oil
fresh country bread,
  sliced

Preparation time: 30 minutes
  (plus cooking time)
Per portion approx.
  190 kcal/790 kJ
14 g P, 25 g F, 26 g CH

1 Wash and dry the peppers. Peel the onion. Wash and dry the aubergines and courgettes. Wash the tomatoes, then remove their stems. Dice the vegetables and chop the onions.

2 Heat the oil in a frying pan and sauté the peppers for 5 minutes. Add the aubergines and cook for a further 5 minutes. Add the courgettes and cook for another 3 minutes. Add the tomatoes and simmer the vegetable mixture for approx. 15 minutes. Season to taste and stir in the chopped herbs.

3 Divide the ratatouille between 4 small bowls. Slice and roll up the lomo, then skewer onto a slice of bread along with 1 sundried tomato. Serve with the ratatouille.

Chicken breast
with ham

Serves 8

2 chicken breast fillets
salt
pepper
1 tbsp curry powder
2 tbsp olive oil
4 slices cooked ham
4 slices hard cheese
4 slices country bread
4 iceberg lettuce leaves
6 tbsp mayonnaise
4 slices raw ham

Preparation time: 30 minutes
Per portion approx.
  157 kcal/659 kJ
5 g P, 11 g F, 8 g CH

1 Wash the chicken breasts, dab dry, season with salt and pepper, sprinkle with curry powder, then brush with olive oil. Cook in a pre-heated oven at 150 °C (Gas Mark 2, fan oven 130 °C) for approx. 25 minutes, brushing frequently with oil. Reduce the temperature by 10 °C for the last 10 minutes of cooking time.

2 Remove the chicken breasts from the oven, then cut lengthways down the middle of each one without slicing all the way through. Insert 2 slices of ham and cheese into each breast and fold over. Wrap in aluminium foil and cook in the oven for a further 20 minutes.

3 Remove the chicken from the foil and cut each breast into 4 sections. Cut each bread slice in half and top with half a lettuce leaf, a little mayonnaise and a piece of stuffed chicken breast, then secure with a wooden skewer, topped with half a slice of raw ham for garnish. Serve warm or cold.

Chicken breast
with chilli

Serves 8

450 g chicken breast fillets

2 onions

4 garlic cloves

1 red chilli pepper

4 tbsp olive oil

2 tsp mild paprika powder

juice of 1 lemon

4 tbsp chopped chervil

salt

pepper

100 g chorizo, sliced

8 lettuce leaves

ciabatta

Preparation time: 20 minutes
  (plus cooking time)
Per portion approx.
  220 kcal/920 kJ
18 g P, 10 g F, 15 g CH

1 Wash the chicken breasts, pat dry and cut into chunks about 2 cm thick. Peel and chop the onions and garlic. Wash and de-seed the chilli pepper, then slice into thin rings.

2 Heat the oil in a frying pan. Fry the meat in hot oil with the onions, garlic, chilli pepper and paprika powder for approx. 3 minutes, stirring frequently.

3 Stir in the lemon juice and chervil, then season all the ingredients with salt and pepper. Skewer the meat onto slices of ciabatta with a slice of chorizo and a lettuce leaf.

Fruits
wrapped in bacon

Serves 8

2 pears

2 peaches

2 bananas

8–12 slices bacon

1 baguette

fat, for greasing

Preparation time: 10 minutes
  (plus baking time)
Per portion approx.
  110 kcal/460 kJ
2 g P, 4 g F, 16 g CH

1 Wash, peel and core the pears, then cut into slices. Wash and peel the peaches, remove the stones and cut into slices. Peel the bananas and cut into bite-sized pieces. Cut the bacon slices in half or quarters, then wrap a slice of bacon around each piece of fruit.

2 Pre-heat the oven to 200 °C (Gas Mark 6, fan oven 180 °C). Grease a baking tray. Arrange the fruit on the tray and bake in the oven until the bacon is crisp. If so desired, cook a few extra bacon slices in the oven. Thread the fruit and bacon onto slices of baguette, then garnish with the extra bacon.

Carrot and ginger soup
with prawns

Serves 4

500 g carrots
1 onion
2–3 cm fresh ginger
2 tbsp butter
100 ml orange juice
750 ml chicken stock
4 king prawns, ready to cook
1–2 tbsp olive oil
salt
pepper
1 tbsp lime juice
pinch chilli powder
½ tsp curry powder
100 g crème fraîche
1 tbsp freshly chopped
   coriander

Preparation time: 20 minutes
   (plus cooking time)
Per portion approx.
   220 kcal/919 kJ
5 g P, 18 g F, 9 g CH

1 Peel the carrots and onions, then roughly chop both vegetables. Peel and finely chop the ginger.

2 Melt the butter in a saucepan, then sauté the carrots, onions and ginger over a moderate heat for approx. 5–10 minutes, stirring constantly. Pour in the orange juice and chicken stock, then simmer for 15–20 minutes over a moderate heat.

3 Make a cut lengthways along the back of the prawns and devein. Wash the prawns and pat dry. Heat the oil in a frying pan, then sear the prawns over a high heat for a few minutes on all sides. Season with salt and pepper, drizzle with lime juice, then remove the pan from the heat.

4 Purée the soup vegetables and season to taste with salt, pepper, chilli and curry powder. Stir in the crème fraîche. Serve the soup sprinkled with freshly chopped coriander and garnish each portion with a prawn.

Pea cappucino
with mint

Serves 4

400 g peas, frozen
2 potatoes
450 ml vegetable stock
200 ml cream
salt
green pepper
1 dash hot pepper sauce
100 g natural yoghurt
2 tbsp milk
4 tbsp chopped mint
1 generous dash mint
  liqueur
4 sprigs mint

Preparation time: 10 minutes
  (plus cooking time)
Per portion approx.
  316 kcal/1321 kJ
7 g P, 18 g F, 21 g CH

1 Tip the frozen peas into a saucepan. Wash, peel and finely dice the potatoes. Add the potatoes and vegetable stock to the peas, bring to a boil and simmer for approx. 15–20 minutes. Whisk the cream until stiff.

2 Remove the saucepan from the heat and purée the soup. Season to taste with salt, pepper and hot pepper sauce. Mix the yoghurt and milk together, then add to the soup. Season the soup once more and stir in the chopped mint and mint liqueur.

3 Serve the soup garnished with a dollop of cream and a mint leaf.

Egg and cream soup
Tuscan-style

Serves 4

4 egg yolks

500 ml chicken stock

2 cl Marsala

¼ tsp ground cinnamon

salt

50 g butter

pinch of sugar

freshly grated nutmeg

Preparation time: 5 minutes
  (plus cooking time)
Per portion approx.
  224 kcal/937 kJ
6 g P, 19 g F, 15 g CH

1 Break the egg yolks into a bowl and gradually whisk in the chicken stock. Pour the Marsala into a bowl and stir in the cinnamon and a pinch of salt.

2 Strain the egg-and-stock mixture through a sieve straight into a saucepan (or into a bowl which should then be placed in a bain-marie). Heat slowly and carefully (ensuring the liquid does not boil), stirring vigorously. Gradually stir in the butter, a little at a time.

Artichokes
with herb-and-egg vinaigrette

Serves 4

4 large artichokes
4 tbsp lemon juice or
  vinegar
1 carrot
2 anchovy fillets
1 small jar capers
2 hard-boiled eggs
1 bunch chives
1 bunch flat-leaf parsley
6 tbsp white wine vinegar
1 tbsp coarse-grained
  mustard
12 tbsp safflower oil
salt
pepper, freshly milled

Preparation time: 15 minutes
  (plus cooking time)
Per portion: approx.
  293 kcal/1231 kJ
1 g P, 31 g F, 3 g CH

1 Rinse the artichokes thoroughly in running water. Remove the outer leaves and cut the stem as short as possible. Using a sharp knife, cut off the artichokes tips – about one third of the overall artichoke – as this will reduce the cooking time. Cook for approx. 25 minutes in boiling water, to which lemon juice or vinegar has been added.

2 Peel the carrot and drain the anchovy fillets and capers. Finely chop the eggs, anchovies and capers. Wash and dry the chives, slice into fine rings. Finely chop the parsley and thoroughly mix all the ingredients with the wine vinegar, mustard, oil, salt and pepper.

3 Once the artichokes are ready (test by pulling off one leaf: if it pulls away easily, the artichoke is cooked), remove from the water and leave to drain upside down on a towel or in a colander. Arrange on plates and serve the vinaigrette dressing separately.

Elegant and festive

Parma ham
with melon

Serves 4

1 honeydew melon

125 g Parma ham, thinly
  sliced

2 tomatoes

½ bunch flat-leaf parsley

½ bunch basil

100 ml olive oil

50 ml wine vinegar

salt

pepper

Preparation time: 30 minutes
Per portion approx.
  347 kcal/1459 kJ
8 g P, 38 g F, 5 g CH

1 Cut the melon in half, scoop out the seeds, then, using a sharp knife, cut the melon into thin wedges, slicing the fruit from the rind. Arrange the melon segments and Parma ham decoratively on plates.

2 Make an X-shaped cut in the tomatoes and plunge in hot water. Peel off the skins, remove the stalks and seeds, then finely dice. Wash and dry the herbs, tear the leaves off the stems and chop.

3 Combine the olive oil, vinegar, tomatoes and herbs to make a dressing, season with salt and pepper. Pour the dressing over the ham and serve.

Elegant and festive

Veal carpaccio
with porcini mushrooms

Serves 4

400 g veal fillet, frozen
salt
pepper
2 tbsp white wine vinegar
2 tbsp lemon juice
5 tbsp olive oil
½ tsp each freshly chopped
 rosemary and thyme
a few leaves curly endive
 lettuce
2 red onions
100 g small porcini
 mushrooms

Preparation time: 15 minutes
Per portion approx.
 257 kcal/1079 kJ
21 g P, 18 g F, 2 g CH

1 Cut the veal into wafer-thin slices. Season with salt and pepper and arrange on plates. Prepare a dressing by combining the vinegar, lemon juice, oil, herbs, salt and pepper, then drizzle two-thirds of the sauce over the slices of veal.

2 Wash the salad leaves, shake them dry, then scatter over the sliced meat. Peel and very finely chop the onions.

3 Clean the mushrooms and wipe with a damp cloth, then slice very finely and place over the curly endive leaves. Season with salt and pepper, drizzle with the remaining dressing and sprinkle with onions.

Salmon rolls
with trout caviar

Serves 4

100 g low-fat quark

salt

pepper

2 tbsp freshly grated
  horseradish

small amount of milk or
  cream

1 bunch dill

1 cucumber

a few leaves oakleaf lettuce

8 slices smoked salmon

4 tbsp caviar (trout caviar)

1 lime, to garnish

Preparation time: 20 minutes
Per portion approx.
  157 kcal/659 kJ
20 g P, 7 g F, 4 g CH

1 Season the quark with salt and pepper, stir in the horseradish and a little milk or cream, then mix until smooth and creamy. Wash the dill, shake it dry, reserve a few sprigs for garnish then finely chop the leaves. Stir the chopped dill into the mixture.

2 Peel the cucumber. Slice one third of the cucumber into thin strips, then dice the remainder. Wash the oakleaf lettuce, shake it dry and cut into strips.

3 Cut the slices of smoked salmon in half and spread with the horseradish-and-quark mixture. Place strips of lettuce and cucumber on each piece of salmon and roll up. Arrange the salmon rolls in a dish sprinkled with chopped cucumber. Spoon the trout caviar over the top. If so desired, garnish with slices of lime and dill before serving.

Prawns with pastis
and fennel

Serves 4

600 g fresh (or frozen)
  prawns, heads removed,
  tails intact
3 fennel bulbs
5 shallots
1 tbsp + 150 g ice-cold
  butter
salt
pepper
2 tbsp oil
5 tbsp pastis liqueur
150 ml fish stock (bottled)

Preparation time: 20 minutes
  (plus cooking time)
Per portion approx.
  570 kcal/2394 kJ
30 g P, 39 g F, 8 g CH

1 Rinse the prawns thoroughly and pat dry. Wash the fennel, finely chop the green leaves and set aside. Finely slice the fennel bulbs. Peel and finely dice the shallots.

2 Melt 1 tablespoon of butter in a frying pan and sauté the fennel with half the diced shallots. Add 5–6 tablespoons of water, cover with a lid and simmer for 8–10 minutes. Season with salt and pepper.

3 Meanwhile, heat the oil in another frying pan and sauté the prawns and the remaining shallots for 2–3 minutes, turning frequently. Season with salt and pepper, remove from the pan, cover and keep warm.

4 Stir the pastis and fish stock into the leftover cooking juices, then cook over a high heat until the liquid has reduced by half. Reduce the heat. Cut the cold butter into small pieces. Whisk these into the hot (but no longer bubbling) sauce and cook over a low heat until it turns smooth and creamy. Season to taste, divide into portions and sprinkle with chopped fennel to garnish. Oven-baked potatoes make an excellent accompaniment to this dish.

Salmon and spinach parcels
with capers

Serves 4

250 g leaf spinach

500 g potatoes

600 g salmon fillet (skinned)

2 sprigs parsley

2 sprigs basil

3 shallots

3 tbsp salted capers
(or preserved in a jar)

3 tbsp butter

1 garlic bulb

1 unwaxed lime

salt

pepper

Preparation time: 30 minutes
(plus cooking time)
Per portion approx.
470 kcal/1974 kJ
33 g P, 29 g F, 16 g CH

1 Wash the spinach and leave to drain thoroughly or spin dry.

2 Peel and wash the potatoes, then parboil for approx. 15 minutes in lightly salted water. Drain and slice thinly. Rinse the salmon, pat dry and divide into 4 pieces.

3 Wash and dry the parsley and basil, then finely chop the leaves. Peel and finely dice the shallots. Rinse the capers, drain thoroughly and roughly chop. Combine all the ingredients with the butter and knead together. Split the garlic bulb apart and peel each clove. Wash the lime in hot water, pat dry and cut into slices.

4 Pre-heat the oven to 200 °C (Gas Mark 6, fan oven 180 °C). Set out 4 large sheets of greaseproof or baking paper. Place potato slices in the middle of each one and season with salt and pepper. Arrange the spinach and a piece of salmon on top of the potatoes, then dot with herb-and-caper butter. Top each portion with slices of lime and a quarter of the garlic cloves.

5 Seal the salmon parcels closed by folding the top edges of the paper together, making sure that the sides are also well sealed. Bake in the oven for approx. 20 minutes. Remove the paper and serve immediately.

Elegant and festive

Monkfish
with olive sauce

Serves 4

2 unwaxed lemons
1 sprig rosemary
1 tsp sea salt
4 monkfish fillets (approx.
   200 g each)
200 g black olives (pitted)
½ red chilli pepper
½ bunch each basil,
   marjoram and parsley
tender celery leaves
1 garlic clove
8 tbsp olive oil
pepper
balsamic vinegar
150 g rucola
salt

Preparation time: 20 minutes
   (plus marinating and cooking
   time)
Per portion approx.
   400 kcal/1680 kJ
38 g P, 26 g F, 1 g CH

1 Wash and dry the lemons, then finely grate the peel. Squeeze the juice from the lemons and set aside. Wash the rosemary and shake dry. Tear off the leaves, sprinkle with salt and lemon zest, and crush to a paste using a pestle and mortar. Rinse the fish, pat dry and coat with the lemon-and-rosemary paste. Wrap the fish in aluminium foil and place in the fridge to marinate for 1 hour.

2 Roughly chop the olives. Cut the chilli pepper in half lengthways, de-seed and chop. Wash the herbs and celery leaves, shake dry, then chop. Peel and finely chop the garlic. Stir in 3 tablespoons of olive oil and 4–5 tablespoons of lemon juice. Season to taste with pepper and balsamic vinegar.

3 Pre-heat the oven to 200 °C (Gas Mark 6, fan oven 180 °C). Remove the fish fillets from the fridge and dab off the marinade. Brush the fish with a little olive oil. Heat a large, ovenproof roasting pan, adding 1–2 tablespoons of olive oil. Fry the fish for approx. 2 minutes each side, then continue cooking in the oven for approx. 7 minutes.

4 Wash the rucola, then shake dry. Place in a bowl and add the dressing, made by blending the remaining olive oil, a little lemon juice, salt and pepper. Place the rucola and fish on pre-warmed plates and dress with the olive-and-chilli mixture. Potato purée makes an excellent companion to this dish.

Veal breast
stuffed with pork fillet

Serves 4

100 g each of calf's brains
  and sweetbreads
15 g dried porcini
  mushrooms
1 garlic clove
750 g veal breast with a
  pocket cut into it
100 g pork fillet
30 g butter
200 ml white wine
75 g peas
1 tbsp chopped marjoram
2 tbsp chopped pistachios
3 tbsp grated Parmesan
3 eggs
2 l vegetable stock

Preparation time: 45 minutes
  (plus soaking and cooking time)
Per portion approx.
  440 kcal/1848 kJ
48 g P, 25 g F, 4 g CH

1 Soak the calf's brain and sweetbreads for 2 hours, changing the water occasionally, then clean and rinse. Soak the porcini mushrooms in cold water. Peel the garlic cloves, then rub the veal breast with the garlic. Cut the pork fillet into chunks. Heat the butter and sauté the pork fillet. Add the calf's brains and sweetbreads, and continue to cook. Pour in the white wine.

2 Drain and finely chop the porcini mushrooms, then cook with the above ingredients for 2 minutes. Purée all the ingredients. Work the puréed meat mixture into a smooth paste along with the peas, marjoram, pistachios, Parmesan and eggs. Stuff the mixture into the veal breast and secure with kitchen twine.

3 Place the veal breast in a large saucepan with the vegetable stock, then cover and simmer for approx. 10 minutes. Remove the lid and cook for a further hour. Remove the veal from the pan, pierce the meat several times and leave to cool between two plates. When ready to serve, slice the meat and garnish with an oil-and-herb sauce.

Veal ragout
with rosemary

Serves 4

700 g veal

3 tbsp olive oil

1 onion

2 garlic cloves

1 tbsp each chopped
   rosemary and sage

1 bay leaf

200 g tomatoes

125 ml dry white wine

50 g green olives, pitted

1 tbsp capers

2 anchovies

salt

pepper

Preparation time: 30 minutes
   (plus cooking time)
Per portion approx.
   290 kcal/1218 kJ
37 g P, 11 g F, 5 g CH

1 Cut the veal into cubes. Heat the oil in a frying pan, then sear the meat quickly over a high heat. Remove the meat from the pan. Peel and chop the onion and garlic, then fry gently in the leftover oil in the pan along with the rosemary, sage and bay leaf.

2 Make a cross-shaped cut in the tomatoes, plunge briefly in boiling water, rinse in cold water, then peel off the skins and dice. Add to the frying pan, along with the cubed veal, white wine, olives and capers. Chop the anchovies, then add to the frying pan. Cover and simmer for approx. 40 minutes. Serve with white bread.

Larded roast leg of lamb
with anchovies

Serves 4–5

1 leg of lamb (approx. 1.5 kg)
4–6 garlic cloves
30 g anchovies
pepper
salt
2 tbsp hot, coarse-grained
  mustard
2 tbsp herbes de Provence

Preparation time: 15 minutes
  (plus cooking time)
Per portion approx.
  615 kcal/2583 kJ
65 g P, 37 g F, 2 g CH

1 Pre-heat the oven to 150 °C (Gas Mark 2, fan oven 130 °C). Wash the leg of lamb and pat dry. Peel the garlic cloves and slice lengthways. Rinse the anchovies and cut in half.

2 Using a sharp knife, cut slits in the leg of lamb on all sides, then stick pieces of garlic clove and anchovy into each slit. Season the meat well with pepper and salt, brush with mustard, then sprinkle with herbs.

3 Place the leg of lamb in a roasting tin, add a cup of water and roast for approx. 2–3 hours in the oven, basting the meat regularly with cooking juices. If necessary, add a little more hot water to the roasting pan. Green beans and Duchesse potatoes make good accompaniments to this dish.

Oven-baked fillet of beef
with herbs

Serves 4–5

600 g beef fillet
2 tbsp oil
salt
pepper
1 bunch parsley
1 bunch chives
1 bunch basil
300 g kohlrabi
300 g carrots
150 g sugar snap peas
1 tbsp butter
1 pinch vegetable stock
  granules
fat, for greasing

Preparation time: 45 minutes
  (plus cooking time)
Per portion approx.
  620 kcal/2604 kJ
45 g P, 33 g F, 32 g CH

1 Wash the fillet of beef and pat dry. Pre-heat the oven to 200 °C (Gas Mark 6, fan oven 180 °C). Heat the oil in a roasting tin or ovenproof pan. Sear the fillet of beef all over in hot oil for 5–8 minutes over a high heat. Season with salt and pepper. Place in the oven and roast for 25–30 minutes.

2 Wash the herbs, shake them dry, then chop and sprinkle over a shallow platter. Cover and set aside. Wash the kohlrabi and carrots, then dice finely. Wash the sugar snap peas and cut diagonally into 2–3 strips.

3 Melt the butter in a saucepan. Sauté the vegetables over a moderate heat for 3 minutes. Add 100 ml water and the stock, cover and gently cook all the ingredients for 5–6 minutes.

4 Remove the fillet from the oven, toss the meat in the reserved herbs, wrap in aluminium foil and leave to absorb the flavours for approx. 10 minutes. Remove the foil and cut into slices. Serve with the vegetables. Gratin potatoes also go very well with this dish.

Braised rabbit
with sultanas

Serves 4

4 rabbit legs (250 g each)
salt
pepper
2 onions
2 garlic cloves
1 bunch parsley
2 tbsp oil
2 bay leaves
2 tsp mild paprika powder
1 sachet saffron strands (1 g)
100 ml dry sherry
50 g sultanas
200 ml chicken stock
1 tin chick peas (425 g)

Preparation time: 30 minutes
  (plus cooking time)
Per portion approx.
  372 kcal/1562 kJ
43 g P, 10 g F, 21 g CH

1 Wash the rabbit legs, pat dry, then rub all over with salt and pepper. Peel and finely dice the onions. Peel and finely slice the garlic cloves. Wash the parsley, shake dry and chop the leaves.

2 Heat the oil in a frying pan, then sear the rabbit legs quickly on all sides in the hot oil. Add the onions and garlic, and fry for a further 2 minutes. Add the bay leaves, paprika powder and saffron strands, then pour in the sherry. Add the sultanas and chicken stock, bring to a boil, then cover and simmer over a moderate heat for approx. 1 hour.

3 Rinse the chick peas in a sieve, then allow to drain. Add to the frying-pan 10 minutes before the end of cooking time. Season all the ingredients with salt and pepper, and sprinkle with plenty of parsley.

Italian-style cabbage soup
with fontina cheese

Serves 4

1 medium Savoy cabbage
salt
250 g day-old white bread
100 g butter
approx. 800 ml vegetable
  stock
250 g fontina cheese, sliced
white pepper
butter, for greasing

Preparation time: 20 minutes
  (plus cooking and baking time)
Per portion approx.
  690 kcal/2884 kJ
30 g P, 41 g F, 39 g CH

1 Clean the Savoy cabbage, removing the dark-green, outer leaves. Cut the cabbage in half, then into quarters and remove the stalk. Slice the leaves into fine strips. Wash, then parboil in plenty of boiling, salted water for approx. 10 minutes. Drain, rinse briefly in cold water, then leave to drain.

2 Pre-heat the oven to 220 °C (Gas Mark 6, fan oven 200 °C). Slice the white bread. Grease a large baking dish with a little butter. Arrange a layer of bread slices on the base of the dish and spoon 3 tablespoons of vegetable stock over the top. Add a layer of cabbage, dotting 2 tablespoons of butter over the top, and cover with sliced cheese. Repeat these layers until all the ingredients are used up, finishing with a layer of sliced bread.

3 Pour the rest of the stock over the top and dot with the remaining butter.

4 Place the soup in the oven and cook for approx. 25 minutes until the bread turns golden brown. Season with salt and pepper.

French onion soup
with double cream

Serves 4

4–5 onions (approx. 400 g)
3 garlic cloves
2 tbsp butter
1.5 l vegetable stock
pepper
4 slices rye bread
400 g Gruyère, sliced
100 g double cream

Preparation time: 15 minutes
  (plus cooking time)
Per portion approx.
  380 kcal/1588 kJ
15 g P, 17 g F, 35 g CH

1 Peel and finely slice the onions and garlic. Melt the butter in a large saucepan, then sauté the onions and garlic over a moderate heat for approx. 8 minutes until golden brown. Add the stock, cover and simmer the onions over a low heat for approx. 20 minutes. Season with pepper.

2 Pre-heat the oven to 150 °C (Gas Mark 2, fan oven 130 °C). Toast the slices of bread, then cut in half. Arrange alternating layers of bread and cheese in ovenproof soup bowls, then add the onion soup. Place the bowls in the oven for approx. 10 minutes. Spoon a dollop of double cream into each portion of soup just before serving.

Chorizo stew
with potatoes

Serves 4

1 red, 1 green and 1 yellow
  bell pepper
2–3 garlic cloves
4 onions
1 kg potatoes
250 g chorizo sausage
3 tbsp olive oil
1 sachet saffron strands
1 bay leaf
750 ml vegetable stock
salt
pepper

Preparation time: 15 minutes
  (plus cooking time)
Per portion approx.
  580 kcal/2424 kJ
20 g P, 31 g F, 45 g CH

1 Cut the bell peppers in half and de-seed, removing the white pith, then wash and cut into strips.
Peel and very finely chop the garlic. Peel the onions
and cut into segments. Peel and wash the potatoes,
then cut into bite-sized chunks. Cut the rind off the
chorizo, then slice up the sausage.

2 Heat the olive oil in a saucepan over a moderate heat. Add the strips of bell pepper, sauté for
5 minutes, stirring constantly, then remove from the
saucepan. Add the onions and chorizo to the saucepan, then cook for 3 minutes before adding the garlic
and frying for a further 1–2 minutes. Add the potatoes, saffron and bay leaf, then pour in the vegetable
stock.

3 Bring all the ingredients to a boil, then cover
and simmer over a moderate heat for approx.
20 minutes. Return the bell peppers to the saucepan
and simmer for a further 5 minutes. Season the stew
with salt and pepper.

Classic lasagne
with red wine

Serves 4

100 g streaky bacon
1 tbsp olive oil
1 onion
2 garlic cloves
350 g minced meat
   (pork and beef)
salt
pepper
paprika powder
150 ml red wine
500 g tinned chopped
   tomatoes
2 tbsp butter
2 tbsp flour
500 ml milk
nutmeg
500 g lasagne sheets (no
   pre-cooking required)
100 g Parmesan, freshly
   grated
fat, for greasing

Preparation time: 30 minutes
Per portion approx.
   1125 kcal/4725 kJ
45 g P, 64 g F, 91 g CH

1 Finely dice the bacon. Heat the oil in a large frying pan and fry the bacon until the fat begins to melt. Peel and finely chop the onions and garlic cloves, then fry with the bacon.

2 Add the minced meat and cook, stirring constantly, until the meat is crumbly. Season with salt, pepper and paprika powder, then pour in the red wine. Add the tinned tomatoes with their juices and simmer all the ingredients for 10–15 minutes.

3 Make a roux from the melted butter and flour, then stir in the milk. Bring to a boil, stirring constantly until creamy, then season with salt, pepper and nutmeg. Remove from the heat. Pre-heat the oven to 180 °C (Gas Mark 4, fan oven 160 °C).

4 Pour a little of the béchamel sauce into a greased baking dish. Add alternating layers of lasagne sheets, meat sauce and béchamel sauce until all the ingredients are used up.

5 Sprinkle grated cheese over the top, then cover and bake in the oven for approx. 20 minutes. Uncover and leave in the oven to cook for a further 10 minutes. Serve with a salad.

Polenta al forno
with fonlina cheese

Serves 4

10 g dried porcini
 mushrooms
300 g polenta
salt
400 g tomatoes
1 tbsp butter
75 g streaky bacon, diced
1 onion
2 carrots
1 stick celery
1 sausage
200 g minced beef
50 ml red wine
100 g fontina cheese
50 g Parmesan
3 tbsp butter
fat, for greasing

Preparation time: 40 minutes
 (plus time for soaking, cooking
 and baking)
Per portion approx.
 1067 kcal/4481 kJ
37 g P, 73 g F, 63 g CH

1 Soak the porcini mushrooms in water, drain, then chop into small pieces. Cook the polenta in 1 litre of gently boiling, salted water over a low temperature for approx. 20 minutes. Using a palette knife, spread the polenta over a wooden board and leave to cool.

2 Cut a cross into the stalk area of each tomato, plunge in boiling, salted water, douse with cold water, peel off the skins, dice and remove the seeds. Set aside.

3 Melt the butter in a frying pan, then fry the diced bacon until the fat begins to run. Peel and chop the onion, then add to the pan. Wash, peel and dice the carrots and celery. Add both vegetables to the frying pan and cook for a further 3 minutes.

4 Dice the sausage, then add to the frying pan along with the minced beef and porcini mushrooms. Stir in the tomatoes and red wine, season to taste and cook until the liquid reduces a little. Cut the cheese into slices and grate the Parmesan.

5 Pre-heat the oven to 200 °C (Gas Mark 6, fan oven 180 °C) and grease a baking dish. Cut the polenta into strips approx. 5 cm wide, then arrange in the dish with alternating layers of minced beef and cheese slices. Dot butter over the top and sprinkle with Parmesan. Bake in the oven for approx. 35 minutes.

Bucatini
in Gorgonzola sauce

Serves 4
150 g Gorgonzola
250 ml cream
salt
pepper
sugar
150 g Parma ham, sliced
400 g bucatini
1 bunch parsley

Preparation time: 25 minutes
Per portion approx.
 905 kcal/3801 kJ
35 g P, 46 g F, 87 g CH

1 Cut the rind off the Gorgonzola, then dice the cheese and melt in a saucepan over a low heat, stirring gently.

2 Stir in the cream and season with salt, pepper and a small pinch of sugar. Cook for approx. 4 minutes, stirring constantly.

3 Cut each slice of Parma ham in half and add to the cheese sauce. Cook the bucatini in plenty of salted water, according to the instructions on the packet.

4 Wash and dry the parsley, then finely chop the leaves. Pour the cooked bucatini into a colander and allow to drain. Mix with the Gorgonzola sauce and serve sprinkled with chopped parsley.

Fondue bourguignonne
with watercress sauce

Serves 6
For the meat:
150–200 g meat per person

In total:
250–300 g fillet of beef
250–300 g fillet of lamb
250–300 g fillet of pork
250–300 g chicken breast
1 l peanut oil or 1 kg
   coconut oil
salt
pepper

For the watercress-and-lemon sauce:
6 tbsp mayonnaise
1 dash of lemon juice
2–3 tbsp watercress, finely
   chopped
1 tbsp diced lemon
   segments
white pepper

Preparation time: 45 minutes
Per portion: approx.
   396 kcal/1663 kJ
49 g P, 19 g F, 6 g CH

1 Wash the meat, pat dry, then cut into cubes, 2 cm thick, and arrange on a platter. Place the *réchaud* (burner) in the centre of the table, then heat the oil or coconut oil in the fondue pot and adjust the flame so that the oil continues to bubble gently throughout the meal.

2 Thread a piece of meat on a fondue fork and place in the hot oil, leaving the meat to cook until it is done to suit each guest's taste. Season with salt and pepper, then dip into one of the accompanying sauces and enjoy.

3 A colourful, mixed salad and bread make good accompaniments to this type of fondue, and potato batons may also be provided to be cooked along with the meat.

4 To make the watercress-and-lemon sauce: thoroughly mix all the ingredients together and garnish with a few watercress leaves.

Cheese fondue
with kirsch

Serves 4

white bread and/or baby
  potatoes
1 garlic clove
650 ml dry white wine
600 g Gruyère
300 g Emmental
125 ml kirsch liqueur
3 tsp cornstarch
pepper

Preparation time: 40 minutes
Per portion: approx.
  1065 kcal/4473 kJ
65 g P, 68 g F, 3 g CH

1 Add the potatoes to a saucepan of boiling water and cook for approx. 20 minutes until tender. Cut the bread into bite-sized chunks and place in a bread basket or bowl to serve.

2 Peel and cut the garlic clove in half and rub the halves around the inside of the fondue pot. Add the wine to the pot, then heat on the hob over a low heat. Grate the two types of cheese. Gradually stir the grated cheese into the wine, adding small amounts at a time and stirring constantly until it is melted. Keep stirring, making sure that the cheese at the base of the pot is kept moving to prevent sticking.

3 Mix the kirsch and cornstarch together to form a smooth paste, then stir into the cheese fondue mixture. Transfer the fondue pot to the table, placing it on the *réchaud* over a small flame. Serve with the potatoes and cubes of bread.

4 Gherkins, silver onions, olives, dried tomatoes, anchovies, mild, preserved chilli peppers, prawns, mushrooms, asparagus tips, mini corn cobs and fresh fruit are all ideal ingredients to serve with cheese fondue.

Paella

Spanish rice platter

Serves 4

200 g squid rings, frozen
1 onion
2 garlic cloves
2 small, red chilli peppers
1 red and 1 green bell
  pepper
4 chicken drumsticks
salt
black pepper
pinch of ground paprika
200 g chorizo (or spicy
  cured sausage)
4 tbsp olive oil
250 g parboiled rice
100 ml white wine
1 sachet saffron (0.2 g)
approx. 500 ml meat stock
1 unwaxed lemon

Preparation time: 30 minutes
  (plus defrosting and cooking
  time)
Per portion approx.
  850 kcal/3550 kJ
51 g P, 43 g F, 59 g CH

1 Defrost the squid rings. Peel and finely chop the onion and garlic cloves. Wash the chilli and bell peppers, pat dry, then cut in half lengthways and remove the seeds. Finely dice the chilli peppers, then cut the bell peppers into 1-cm pieces.

2 Rinse the chicken legs in running cold water, pat dry and then rub with salt, pepper and paprika powder. Skin and slice the chorizo sausage.

3 Heat the oil in a large, deep frying pan. Add the chicken drumsticks, sear over a high heat for approx. 3 minutes on both sides, then remove from the pan. Add the remaining oil to the frying pan, add the diced onions, garlic, chilli and bell peppers, then sauté, stirring constantly. Sprinkle in the rice and cook until translucent.

4 Pour the white wine over the vegetable-and-rice mixture, then stir in the saffron. Season all the ingredients with salt and pepper, pour in approx. 500 ml of meat stock and bring to a boil. Add the chicken legs, then cover with a lid and cook for approx. 15 minutes.

5 If necessary, pour in a little more stock to prevent the rice from burning. Add the defrosted squid rings and sliced chorizo to the paella, then cook all the ingredients for another 15 minutes. Season the paella with salt, pepper and paprika. Wash the lemon, slice into 8 segments and serve with the paella.

Delicious basics

Butter variations
with herb, spice and citrus flavouring

For herb butter

4 sprigs thyme

2 sprigs rosemary

1 bunch chervil

10 stems pimpernel

5 stems lemon balm

1 tsp zest from an unwaxed
lemon

250 g butter, salt

For paprika butter

4 tbsp tomato purée

2 ½ tsp rose paprika

250 g butter

salt, white pepper

1 heaped tsp red peppercorns

For caper butter

50 g capers, 250 g butter

2 tsp orange juice, 1 tsp mustard

salt, white pepper

1 tsp organic orange zest

For lemon butter

1 tsp organic lemon zest

250 g butter

salt, white pepper

2 tbsp chopped mint leaves

Preparation time for each type of
  butter: 10 minutes
Per butter mixture:
  approx. 1853 kcal/7753 kJ
3 g P, 280 g F, 2 g CH

1 To make herb butter, wash and dry the herbs, then tear off the leaves. Mix thoroughly with the lemon zest, soft butter and salt. Place in a sealed container and store in the freezer for up to 3 months. Goes well with meat, poultry and vegetables.

2 To make paprika butter, combine the tomato purée, paprika and soft butter, mixing thoroughly. Season with salt and pepper. Stir in the crushed peppercorns. Place in a sealed container and store in the freezer for up to 3 months. Makes a good accompaniment to beef, pork or lamb.

3 To make caper butter, drain the capers, then very finely chop. Mix with the soft butter, orange juice and mustard. Season with salt and pepper, then stir in the orange zest. Place in a sealed container and store in the freezer for up to 3 months. Goes well with both meat and poultry.

4 To make lemon butter, knead the lemon zest into the soft butter, then season with salt and pepper. Stir in the mint. Place in a sealed container and store in the freezer for up to 3 months. Makes an excellent companion to fish and seafood dishes, veal and poultry.

Pepper salad
with olive breadsticks

Serves 4
2 red, 2 green and
  2 yellow bell peppers
6 tbsp olive oil
3 garlic cloves
2 tbsp chopped oregano
  leaves
150 g sheep's cheese
juice of 1 lime
salt
pepper

For the breadsticks:
150 g puff pastry, frozen
50 g green olives, pitted
1 egg yolk
1 tbsp chopped walnut
  kernels

Preparation time: 40 minutes
  (plus marinating and grilling
  time)
Per portion approx.
  423 kcal/1769 kJ
13 g P, 28 g F, 27 g CH

1 Cut the bell peppers in half, remove the seeds and pith, rinse and pat dry. Cut the peppers into bite-sized pieces. Add the olive oil to a frying pan, a little at a time, and gradually sauté all the peppers over a moderate heat. Remove from the pan and place in a serving bowl.

2 Peel and very thinly slice the garlic cloves. Fry in the remaining oil, then add to the sliced pepper along with the oregano. Dice the sheep's cheese into small cubes and add to the pepper and garlic. Drizzle lime juice over the salad and season with salt and pepper. Cover and leave to marinate in the fridge for 1 hour.

3 To make the breadsticks, defrost the puff pastry. Dust a work surface with flour, then roll out the pastry into a thin square sheet. Very finely chop the olives. Pre-heat the oven to 180 °C (Gas Mark 4, fan oven 160 °C).

4 Lightly beat the egg yolk, then brush the pastry with some of the beaten egg. Sprinkle half the sheet with olives and walnuts, then fold the other half over the top. Press the layers of pastry firmly together, then brush with the remaining egg yolk. Cut the pastry into 20 strips approx. 1 cm wide. Place the breadsticks on a wire tray lined with aluminium foil and bake in the oven for approx. 10 minutes until crisp and golden brown.

Couscous salad
with chilli dressing

Serves 4

200 g couscous

2 garlic cloves

2 onions

1 red, 1 green and
  1 yellow bell pepper

1 cucumber

4 tomatoes

250 g button mushrooms

1 bunch dill

For the dressing:

juice of 1 lemon

3 tbsp rapeseed oil

salt

pepper

½ tsp ground chilli
  powder

1 tbsp sliced chives

Preparation time: 40 minutes
  (plus marinating time)
Per portion approx.
  267 kcal/1119 kJ
12 g P, 3 g F, 55 g CH

1 Prepare the couscous according to the instructions on the packet. Leave to cool, occasionally fluffing up the grains with a fork.

2 Peel the garlic and onions, crush the garlic in a garlic press and finely chop the onions. Cut the bell peppers in half, then wash, dry and dice into small cubes. Thoroughly wash the cucumber, pat dry and slice off the ends. Cut the cucumber in half lengthways and finely slice.

3 Cut a cross in the tomatoes. Plunge briefly in boiling water, then rinse in cold water, peel off the skins and cut out the stalks. Remove the seeds and chop the flesh into small pieces. Clean the button mushrooms, wipe with a damp cloth and, depending on size, cut each one into half or quarters. Wash the dill, shake dry, then snip the tips off the stems and finely chop.

4 In a salad bowl, thoroughly combine the cooled couscous with the garlic, onions, peppers, cucumber, tomatoes, mushrooms and dill.

5 To make the dressing, blend together the lemon juice and oil. Add the salt, pepper and chilli powder, stir in the chives, then mix the dressing and salad ingredients together and leave to marinate for 1 hour.

Chicken hot dogs
with pesto

Serves 4

For the pesto:
1 garlic clove
1 tbsp pine kernels
1 small, red chilli pepper
100 g sundried tomatoes
  in oil
25 g grated Parmesan
50 ml olive oil
1 tbsp chopped dill
salt

Also:
2 onions
3 tbsp rapeseed oil
1 cucumber
1 tbsp chopped dill
1 tsp lemon juice
1 tsp sugar
salt
pepper
4 chicken breast fillets
4 hot dog rolls
2 vine tomatoes

Preparation time: 50 minutes
  (plus cooking time)
Per portion approx.
  446 kcal/1866 kJ
32 g P, 23 g F, 19 g CH

1 To make the pesto, peel the garlic, toast the pine kernels in a dry frying pan until golden brown. Set aside to cool. Wash and roughly chop the chilli pepper. Drain the tomatoes. Purée the garlic, pine kernels, chilli, tomatoes, Parmesan and olive oil together into a coarse paste. Stir the dill into the pesto and season with salt.

2 To make the hot dogs, peel and finely dice the onions. Brown the onions gently in 1 tablespoon of rapeseed oil. Remove from the heat and leave to cool.

3 Wash and peel the cucumber. Using a vegetable peeler, slice the cucumber into long, thin strips. Combine the dill, lemon juice, sugar and 1 tablespoon of rapeseed oil. Coat the cucumber strips with this dressing and season with salt and pepper.

4 Wash the chicken breast, pat dry and cut lengthways into 3–4 strips. Season with salt, brush with the rest of the oil, then cook on a hot barbecue grill for 5 minutes, turning frequently. Slice open the hot dog rolls and grill for a minute on each side.

5 Wash and slice the tomatoes, then place tomato slices on one half of each hot dog roll. Spread with pesto and top with barbecued chicken strips. Top with sliced cucumber and onions, then replace the lid of the hot dog roll.

Creole sausages
with mango relish

Serves 4

For the kebabs:
4 long, thin pork escalopes
  (approx. 200 g each)
2 garlic cloves
8 tbsp rapeseed oil
juice of 1 lime
½ tsp salt
pinch of cayenne pepper,
  grated nutmeg, ground
  cloves, cumin and
  cinnamon
1 tbsp chopped thyme
8 wooden skewers, soaked
  in water

For the relish:
1 ripe mango
2 red chilli peppers
piece of ginger (2 cm)
2 sprigs mint
2 tbsp lime juice
salt, pepper, honey

Preparation time: 30 minutes
  (plus marinating and grilling
  time)
Per portion approx.
  554 kcal/2318 kJ
35 g P, 34 g F, 51 g CH

1 Wash the escalopes, pat dry, then cut in half lengthways. Place in a freezer bag. To make the marinade, peel and finely chop the garlic, then mix with the rest of the ingredients. Rub the marinade into the escalopes, firmly seal the freezer bags, then leave in the fridge to marinate for at least 3 hours.

2 To make the relish, peel the mango, remove the stone, then chop the flesh into small pieces. Cut the chilli peppers in half lengthways, then wash and roughly chop. Peel and chop the ginger, wash and dry the mint, then tear off the leaves. Purée all the ingredients in a blender with the lime juice. Season with salt, pepper and honey.

3 Remove the escalopes from the marinade and allow to drain. Twist the lengths of meat around the skewers. Lightly brush the grill rack with oil. Place the kebabs on the hot barbecue, brush with a little marinade and grill for 10–12 minutes over a moderate heat, turning frequently. Serve immediately with the relish.

Pork and sage medallions
with chutney

Serves 4
For the rhubarb chutney:
1 stick rhubarb
½ tsp grated zest of
  1 unwaxed lemon
1 piece of ginger (2 cm)
45 g brown sugar
20 ml white wine vinegar
pinch of cinnamon
20 g sultanas
salt

For the kebabs:
approx. 800 g pork fillet
pepper
36 fresh sage leaves
12 slices smoked, streaky
  bacon
16 stuffed, green olives
4 tbsp olive oil

Preparation time: 30 minutes
  (plus cooking and grilling time)
Per portion approx.
  862 kcal/3603 kJ
54 g P, 68 g F, 20 g CH

1 To make the chutney, wash the rhubarb, wipe dry, then cut into small pieces. Place the rhubarb in a saucepan along with the lemon zest. Peel and very finely chop the ginger, then add to the saucepan together with all the other chutney ingredients apart from the sultanas and salt. Bring to a boil, stirring constantly and simmer gently for approx. 15 minutes.

2 Add the sultanas and a little salt, then simmer for another 4 minutes. Pour into a bowl or glass and leave to cool.

3 To make the kebabs, trim the pork fillet, rinse in cold water and pat dry. Slice the fillet into 12 medallions, approx. 2 cm thick. Season with pepper.

4 Wash the sage leaves, then dab dry. Place 3 sage leaves on each pork medallion. Wrap a slice of bacon around each medallion. Thread 4 olives on each skewer, alternating with 3 medallions of pork.

5 Brush the kebabs with oil, then cook on a hot barbecue grill for approx. 15 minutes, turning once. Serve with the rhubarb chutney.

Swordfish
with ginger dressing

Serves 4
For the ginger dressing:
½ bunch spring onions
100 g fresh ginger
150 ml light soy sauce
1 tbsp sesame oil

For the swordfish:
4 swordfish steaks
  (150–200 g each)
1 egg white
1 red chilli pepper
180 g sesame seeds

Preparation time: 25 minutes
  (plus grilling time)
Per portion approx.
  589 kcal/2465 kJ
53 g P, 30 g F, 22 g CH

1 To make the dressing, wash then finely chop the spring onions. Peel and finely chop the ginger. Place the spring onions and ginger in a bowl, and combine with the soy sauce and sesame oil.

2 Rinse the swordfish steaks in cold water, then pat dry. Whisk the egg white in a bowl until frothy. Cut the chilli pepper in half, wash and chop very finely.

3 Mix the sesame seeds and chilli together on a large platter. Coat the steaks in the egg white, then toss in the sesame seed and chilli mixture until well coated on all sides.

4 Place the swordfish steaks on an oiled grill rack and barbecue for approx. 5 minutes on each side, basting with dressing from time to time. Pulses (in a lentil salad, for example) go well with this dish.

Sea bass
with salsa fresca

Serves 4

For the salsa fresca:

3 large, beef tomatoes

1 shallot

2 garlic cloves

1 red chilli pepper

juice of 1 lemon

2 tbsp olive oil

salt

pepper

3 tbsp freshly chopped
   coriander

For the fish:

4 sea bass fillets

2 tbsp rapeseed oil

salt

pepper

Preparation time: 20 minutes
   (plus marinating and grilling
   time)
Per portion approx.
   185 kcal/776 kJ
29 g P, 6 g F, 3 g CH

1 To make the salsa, plunge the tomatoes in boiling water, remove their skins, stalks and seeds. Finely chop the flesh.

2 Peel and chop the shallot and garlic cloves. Wash the chilli pepper, cut in half and chop finely. Mix thoroughly with the lemon juice, 2 tablespoons of olive oil, salt, pepper and coriander. Leave to marinate for approx. 20 minutes.

3 Wash the fish fillets, pat dry and brush with rapeseed oil. Season with salt and pepper. Cook over a hot barbecue for approx. 4 minutes on each side. Remove the fish from the grill and serve on plates, garnished with *salsa fresca*.

Monkfish kebabs
with figs

Serves 4

12 monkfish medallions
(prepared by a
fishmonger)
1 shallot
1 garlic clove
1 chilli pepper
3 tbsp sesame oil
3 tbsp soy sauce
pepper
4 large, fresh figs
50 g goat's cheese
16 slices prosciutto

Preparation time: 30 minutes
(plus marinating and grilling
time)
Per portion approx.
311 kcal/1307 kJ
30 g P, 16 g F, 7 g C

1 Wash the monkfish medallions and pat dry. Place in a freezer bag. Peel and finely chop the shallot and garlic cloves. Wash the chilli pepper, cut in half, then chop finely.

2 In a bowl, combine the sesame oil, soy sauce, shallot, garlic and chilli pepper to make a marinade. Pour this over the monkfish medallions. Seal the freezer bag tightly and place in the fridge for 2–3 hours.

3 Sprinkle the monkfish medallions with pepper. Wash and dry the figs, then cut into quarters using a sharp knife. Dice the cheese and insert a piece of cheese into each fig quarter. Wrap each fig quarter in a slice of prosciutto.

4 Thread 3 medallions of fish onto each skewer, alternating with 4 fig-and-bacon quarters. Place on a hot, oiled barbecue grill rack and cook for approx. 4 minutes on each side.

Surf & Turf
with veal and clams

Serves 4

4 veal steaks (100 g each)
16 prawns, ready to cook
16 clams, ready to cook
2 unwaxed limes
8 sage leaves
2 garlic cloves
pepper
50 ml olive oil
4 green and 4 red mild
  chilli peppers
salt
rapeseed oil, for basting
lime wedges, to garnish

Preparation time: 20 minutes
  (plus marinating and grilling
  time)
Per portion approx.
  313 kcal/1310 kJ
33 g P, 16 g F, 4 g CH

1 Wash the steaks and pat dry. Devein and wash the prawns, then pat dry. Rinse the clams and pat dry. Refrigerate the prawns and clams until required.

2 Wash and dry the limes, then finely grate the rind. Squeeze the juice from the fruit. Wash and dry the sage. Cut the unpeeled garlic cloves in half.

3 Place the steaks in a freezer bag. Add the lime zest, sage, garlic, a little pepper and the olive oil. Gently massage the marinade into the steaks and leave for 2 hours, then remove the steaks from the freezer bag and pat dry.

4 Thread 4 prawns and 4 clams onto each skewer and drizzle with half the lime juice. Slice the chilli peppers in half lengthways, de-seed, wash and pat dry.

5 Brush the steaks and peppers with a little rapeseed oil, then place on the hot barbecue grill. Cook for 5 minutes, turn over, then grill for a further 5 minutes. Season with salt and pepper, then drizzle with a little lime juice. Place the prawn-and-clam kebabs on the grill rack and cook for 2 minutes on each side.

6 Arrange the veal steaks, kebabs and chilli peppers on plates and garnish with lime slices.

Sesame and serrano burgers
with aioli

Serves 4
For the minced meat:

1 kg minced beef
1 bunch flat-leaf parsley,
  freshly chopped
2 garlic cloves, finely
  chopped
1 tbsp mustard
salt
pepper
1 tsp paprika powder
2 tbsp rapeseed oil

For the aioli:

2 garlic cloves, chopped
1 red chilli pepper, chopped
75 g mayonnaise
2 tsp paprika powder
sea salt

Also:

2 beef tomatoes
8 sesame buns
8 slices serrano ham
8 slices fontina cheese

Preparation time: 20 minutes
  (plus grilling time)
Per portion approx.
  953 kcal/3985 kJ
67 g P, 60 g F, 29 g CH

1 Combine the minced meat, parsley, garlic, mustard, salt, pepper and paprika powder. Moisten your hands with water, then shape the mixture into 8 flat patties. Brush with a little rapeseed oil and cook on a hot barbecue grill for 5 minutes on each side. Grill the serrano ham for a few minutes until crisp.

2 To make the aioli, mix the garlic and chilli pepper with the mayonnaise, then season with paprika powder and salt. Wash and slice the beef tomatoes.

3 Slice the burger buns in, spread each half with aioli. Place half a slice of ham and cheese on one half, then add a burger and top with another half a slice of ham and cheese. Cook over indirect heat for 3 minutes until the cheese is melted. Top with sliced tomatoes, season with salt and pepper, then sandwich with the other half of the bun and press together firmly.

Fillet steaks
with wasabi

Serves 4
For the steaks:
4 thick beef fillet steaks
  (approx. 180 g each)
2 garlic cloves
4 cm fresh ginger
2 tbsp soy sauce
2 tbsp peanut oil

For the dips:
250 g white radish
4 tbsp rice vinegar
5 tbsp lemon juice
2 tsp grated zest of
  1 unwaxed lemon
1 red chilli pepper
salt
sugar
2 tsp wasabi powder
200 g crème fraîche
50 ml soy sauce

Preparation time: 25 minutes
  (plus marinating and grilling
  time)
Per portion approx.
  671 kcal/2804 kJ
63 g P, 44 g F, 11 g CH

1 Rinse the steaks, then pat dry. Peel and very finely chop the garlic and ginger, then mix with the soy sauce and peanut oil. Rub the steaks thoroughly with this marinade, then place in a freezer bag and refrigerate for at least 3 hours.

2 To make the radish dip, peel and very finely chop the white radish, then mix with the rice vinegar, 4 tablespoons of lemon juice and lemon zest. Cut the chilli pepper in half lengthways and remove the seeds. Wash, pat dry and cut into very thin strips, then add to the radish mixture and season all the ingredients with salt and pepper.

3 To make the wasabi dip, combine the wasabi powder with the remaining lemon juice and a little water, then mix with the crème fraîche. Spoon both dips into small bowls. Fill a third bowl with soy sauce.

4 Brush the hot barbecue rack with oil and cook the steaks for 2 minutes on each side. Cut the steaks into slices and serve with the soy sauce and dips.

Lamb chops
with a honey glaze

Serves 4
75 ml balsamic vinegar
3 tbsp honey
salt
pepper
12 lamb chops
2 tbsp olive oil

Preparation time: 15 minutes
  (plus cooking time)
Per portion approx.
  338 kcal/1417 kJ
58 g P, 10 g F, 3 g CH

1 Stir the honey into the balsamic vinegar and mix well. Season with salt and pepper. Set aside half the mixture.

2 Wash the lamb chops, pat dry, then brush with olive oil. Season with salt and pepper. Place on the hot barbecue grill and cook for approx. 2 minutes on each side. Brush with honey glaze and cook for another minute on each side.

3 Remove the chops from the barbecue and brush with the reserved honey mixture. Wrap in foil and leave for 5 minutes.

4 Divide the lamb chops into portions, then drizzle with the meat juices left in the foil. Serve with chimichurri sauce and fresh bread.

Red pepper and ricotta soup
with honey

Serves 4

4 red bell peppers
2 small onions
2 rosemary sprigs
1 red chilli pepper
2–3 tbsp olive oil
800 ml vegetable stock
250 ml cream
150 g ricotta cheese
salt
pepper
1 tsp honey
2 tbsp finely diced, red
  bell pepper

Preparation time: 15 minutes
  (plus cooking time)
Per portion approx.
  380 kcal/1590 kJ
6 g P, 33 g F, 10 g CH

1 Wash and dice the bell peppers. Peel and finely chop the onions. Rinse the rosemary and pat dry, strip off the leaves and finely chop. Cut the chilli pepper in half, remove the seeds, rinse and very finely chop.

2 In a saucepan, heat the oil over a medium heat. Add the bell peppers, onions and chilli pepper and fry gently for approx. 8 minutes, stirring constantly. Pour in the stock, bring to a boil and simmer over a low heat for 10 minutes.

3 Stir in the cream, remove the saucepan from the heat and purée all the ingredients into a smooth soup. Bring to a boil once more, then remove from the heat.

4 Stir in the ricotta and chopped rosemary, and season the soup with salt, pepper and honey.

5 Serve the soup sprinkled with a garnish of finely diced red pepper.

Chicken curry soup
with chilli gremolata

Serves 4
For the soup:
1 leek
3–4 potatoes
2–3 garlic cloves
1 piece fresh ginger
  (approx. 2 cm)
2 tomatoes
2 tbsp olive oil
2 tbsp curry powder
100 g mango fruit
1 l chicken stock
250 ml cream
200 ml milk
salt
½ lemon
200 g frozen peas

For the gremolata:
1 red bell pepper
2 green chilli peppers
1 bunch mint

Preparation time: 25 minutes
  (plus 40 minutes cooking time)
Per portion approx.
  663 kcal/2773 kJ
15 g P, 35 g F, 68 g CH

1 To make the soup, wash the leek. Dice the white part of the stem and thinly slice the green part. Wash, peel and dice the potatoes. Peel and finely chop the garlic and ginger. Plunge the tomatoes into boiling water for approx. 30 seconds, then douse with cold water and peel off the skins. Cut out the stalk, remove the seeds and dice the flesh.

2 Heat the oil in a saucepan over a medium heat. Add the garlic, ginger and diced white leek, then cook gently for 5 minutes. Add the potatoes and tomatoes, and cook for a further 5 minutes. Sprinkle with curry powder and cook for another 2 minutes, stirring constantly.

3 Dice the mango fruit. Add the stock and mango to the saucepan, then cover and gently simmer all the ingredients for 20–25 minutes.

4 Stir the cream and milk into the soup, then purée all the ingredients, adding a little more chicken stock if the consistency of the soup is too thick. Season with salt and lemon juice. Add the leeks and peas, then simmer for a further 5–10 minutes.

5 To make the gremolata, cut the bell pepper and chilli peppers in half, then wash and finely dice. Wash the mint, shake the leaves dry, then finely chop. Mix all the gremolata ingredients together, then serve with the soup.

Marinated sardines
with lemons

Serves 4

600 g sardines, gutted and
  filleted

4 lemons

2 tbsp olive oil

salt

pepper

2 tbsp chopped parsley

lemon slices and dill
  sprigs, to garnish

Preparation time: 30 minutes
  (plus marinating time)
Per portion approx.
  263 kcal/1105 kJ
30 g P, 9 g F, 11 g CH

1 Wash and descale the sardines, then remove the heads and tails. Carefully remove the backbones, then cut out the fillets using a sharp knife. Rinse well and pat dry.

2 Squeeze the juice from the lemons and pour the juice over the sardines. Cover the sardine fillets with foil and leave to marinate for at least 12 hours.

3 Pour the olive oil into a bowl with a little salt and pepper, mixing well. Remove the sardine fillets from the lemon juice and arrange on a serving platter. Drizzle with the olive oil mixture. Sprinkle with chopped parsley and garnish with lemon slices and dill sprigs. Serve with fresh, white bread.

Vitello tonnato
cooked in wine

Serves 4

250 ml white wine
250 ml meat stock
1 tbsp white wine vinegar
1 carrot
1 stick celery and leek
1 garlic clove
500 g loin veal
1 bay leaf
3 peppercorns
salt
100 g tuna, tinned
2 anchovy fillets, from a jar
125 ml meat cooking stock
1 tbsp lemon juice
75 g mayonnaise
salt
pepper
1 tbsp capers
lettuce leaves, tomato
  quarters and chives, to
  garnish

Preparation time: 35 minutes
  (plus cooking and chilling
  time)
Per portion approx.
  303 kcal/1273 kJ
34 g P, 16 g F, 3 g CH

1 Pour the white wine, meat stock and white wine vinegar into a saucepan. Wash, peel and finely dice the carrot. Wash the celery and leek, then slice into rings. Peel and chop the garlic clove. Add to the white wine stock, with the carrot, leek, celery, veal, bay leaf, salt and peppercorns, then cook for approx. 45 minutes, simmering rather than boiling. Leave the ingredients in the cooking liquid to cool.

2 Drain the tuna. Rinse the anchovy fillets and drain. Purée the tuna in the blender with 150 ml of the cooking juices. Chop the anchovies very finely. Combine the lemon juice, mayonnaise, tuna purée and anchovies. Season with salt and pepper, then stir in the capers.

3 Drain the meat, then carve into thin slices and serve cold with the tuna-and-caper sauce. Garnish with lettuce leaves, tomato quarters and chives.

Prawns
with tomato sauce

Serves 4

1 onion

1 garlic clove

4 tbsp olive oil

¼ chilli pepper

2 bay leaves

100 ml sieved tomatoes
(tinned or in a carton)

1 kg prawns, peeled and
deveined

200 ml white wine

2 tbsp chopped parsley

Preparation time: 30 minutes
(plus cooking time)
Per portion approx.
345 kcal/1449 kJ
51 g P, 9 g F, 5 g C

1 Peel the onion and garlic clove, then sauté gently in hot olive oil. Chop the chilli pepper, then add to the onion along with the bay leaves and continue to cook. Add the sieved tomatoes and simmer all the ingredients for approx. 10 minutes.

2 Wash the prawns, pat dry, add to the sauce and season with salt. Pour in the white wine, then cover and simmer for approx. 10 minutes. Sprinkle with chopped parsley before serving. Serve with white bread.

Info: regardless of whether the recipe refers to them as chillies, chilli peppers, peperoncini or peperoni, it simply means the little green or red varieties of chilli peppers. These can vary considerably in terms of how hot they are. They are always milder if the seeds are removed.

Sardines
with pancetta

Serves 4

1 kg fresh sardines,
  ready to cook
4 tbsp olive oil
coarse-grained sea salt
pepper
4 slices pancetta
3 tbsp freshly chopped
  parsley
lemon wedges, to
  garnish

Preparation time: 15 minutes
  (plus grilling time)
Per portion approx.
  550 kcal/2300 kJ
  49 g P, 40 g F, 12 g CH

1 Wash and, if necessary, descale the sardines, then remove the heads. Pat the fish dry. Pre-heat the oven grill. Brush the fish with olive oil, then rub salt and pepper.

2 Cut the pancetta into strips and wrap a strip around each sardine. Arrange the sardines in an ovenproof baking dish or on a baking tray, and grill on each side for approx. 4 minutes.

3 Sprinkle parsley over the sardines and garnish with lemon wedges. Serve accompanied with fresh bread.

Info: unlike other types of fish, there is no closed season for sardine fishing. Good quality fish is available all year round.

Chicken alla toscana
with cannellini beans

Serves 4

1 chicken (approx. 1.2 kg)
salt
pepper
1 onion
2 red bell peppers
1 garlic clove
15 ml olive oil
300 ml puréed tomatoes
150 ml dry white wine
1 sprig oregano
400 g cannellini beans,
  tinned
3 tbsp grated white bread

Preparation time: 20 minutes
  (plus cooking and grilling time)
Per portion approx.
  685 kcal/2877 kJ
69 g P, 34 g F, 20 g CH

1 Cut the chicken into 8 portions and season with salt and pepper. Peel and slice the onion into rings. Remove the seeds from the bell peppers and slice likewise into rings. Peel and chop the garlic clove.

2 Heat the oil in a large casserole dish and brown the chicken on all sides. Remove the chicken from the dish and keep warm.

3 Sauté the sliced onion, bell pepper rings and garlic in the leftover cooking fat. Return the chicken pieces to the cooking pot, add the tomatoes, wine and oregano. Bring the liquid to a boil, then cover and simmer over a low temperature for approx. 35 minutes. Add the drained beans to the casserole for the last 5 minutes of cooking time. Sprinkle grated bread over the top and bake under a hot grill until golden brown.

Mediterranean chicken
with peppers

Serves 6

2 red and 2 yellow bell
   peppers
4 shallots
3 chicken legs
3 chicken breasts, with
   skin
salt
pepper
8 tbsp olive oil
4 garlic cloves, peeled
300 ml dry white wine
10–15 bay leaves
125 g caper berries
   (or capers)
1 bunch flat-leaf parsley

Preparation time: 30 minutes
   (plus cooking time)
Per portion approx.
   753 kcal/3163 kJ
35 g P, 57 g F, 15 g CH

1 Wash and quarter the bell peppers, then cut each quarter in half across the middle. Peel and quarter the shallots. Wash the chicken legs, pat dry and cut each one into 2 sections. Season with salt and pepper.

2 Pre-heat the oven to 200 °C (Gas Mark 6, fan oven 180 °C). In a large ovenproof casserole dish, heat the oil and sauté the chicken on all sides over a high heat until golden brown. Add the bell peppers and garlic, and fry for a few more minutes, then add salt and a generous amount of pepper, and pour in the white wine. Add the bay leaves and cook in the oven for approx. 35 minutes on the second shelf from the bottom.

3 Drain the caper berries and cut in half lengthways. Wash the parsley, shake dry and roughly chop the leaves. Just before the dish is ready to serve, stir in the caper berries and parsley. A fresh baguette makes the perfect accompaniment to this dish.

Involtini
with chicken livers

Serves 4

8 small veal escalopes

salt

pepper

50 g air-dried ham

100 g chicken livers, chopped

1 tbsp each chopped parsley and thyme

1 garlic clove

3 tbsp grated Parmesan

3 tbsp flour

5 tbsp butter

200 ml dry white wine

Preparation time: 20 minutes
   (plus frying and cooking time)
Per portion approx.
   353 kcal/1482 kJ
38 g P, 16 g F, 6 g CH

1 Wash the veal escalopes, pat dry, then hammer into thin steaks. Season with salt and pepper. Finely dice the ham, then mix with the chicken livers and herbs. Peel and chop the garlic clove, then stir into the meat mixture along with the grated Parmesan.

2 Spread some of the mixture over each escalope, roll up and secure with a wooden cocktail stick. Coat the rolls in flour, tapping off any excess.

3 Heat the butter and sauté the involtini on all sides for approx. 3 minutes. Pour in the white wine and simmer for 20 minutes. Season once more with salt and pepper.

Beef and lamb casserole
Mont Ventoux

Serves 6

150 g smoked, streaky
  bacon
1 large onion
5 garlic cloves
2 sprigs rosemary
10 sprigs thyme
1 handful each green and
  black olives
1 cup dried plums
400 g lean beef
400 g lamb
6 tbsp oil
1 cup unsulphurated
  currants
½ l red wine (Côtes du
  Ventoux or Côtes du
  Rhône)
1 tbsp green pepper
salt
250 ml cream
10 cl Cognac

Preparation time: 35 minutes
  (plus cooking time)
Per portion approx.
  598 kcal/2512 kJ
25 g P, 49 g F, 13 g CH

1 Pre-heat the oven to 200 °C (Gas Mark 6, fan oven 180 °C). Dice the bacon. Peel and finely dice the onion and garlic cloves. Wash the rosemary and thyme and shake dry. Pit the olives, then remove the stones from the dried plums and chop into small pieces.

2 Wash the meat, pat dry, trim and dice. In an ovenproof cooking dish, sauté the meat in hot oil, a portion at a time, until it is browned on all sides. Add the diced bacon and onions then fry, stirring constantly, until translucent.

3 Add the olives, garlic, thyme, rosemary, plums and currants to the meat, and pour in the red wine. Cover with a lid and cook in the pre-heated oven for 40 minutes. Season with green pepper and salt, stir in the cream and Cognac, mixing thoroughly, then return to the oven for a further 20–25 minutes. Curly endive salad and fresh baguette or saffron rice make perfect accompaniments to this dish.

Lamb ragout
alla romana

Serves 6

400 g each breast of lamb
  and lamb shoulder
3 tbsp clarified butter
2 onions
3 garlic cloves
2 sprigs rosemary
2 tbsp white wine vinegar
125 ml dry white wine
3 bay leaves
salt
pepper
lamb stock, as required

Preparation time: 30 minutes
  (plus frying and braising time)
Per portion approx.
  373 kcal/1566 kJ
58 g P, 11 g F, 4 g CH

1 Wash and pat the meat dry, trim off any fat, then cut into cubes. Heat the clarified butter in a frying pan, then sear the meat over a high heat. Remove the meat from the pan and set aside.

2 Peel and chop the onions and garlic cloves. Wash and dry the rosemary, then tear off the leaves.

3 Fry the onions and garlic in the leftover cooking fat until translucent. Return the meat to the pan, then add the white wine vinegar, white wine, rosemary and bay leaves, and season with salt and pepper. Cover and simmer for approx. 1 hour, adding a little lamb stock, if necessary. Serve with white bread.

Bavarian cream
with real vanilla

Serves 4

5 sheets of white gelatine
1 vanilla pod
300 ml milk
3 egg yolks
100 g sugar
300 ml double cream

Preparation time: 25 minutes
  (plus chilling time)
Per portion approx.
  400 kcal/1680 kJ
8 g P, 27 g F, 31 g CH

1 Soak the gelatine in cold water according to the instructions on the packet. Slice open the vanilla pod lengthways, scoop out the pulp and stir into the milk along with the vanilla pod. Bring the milk to a boil, then remove from the heat and take out the pod.

2 Whisk the egg yolks and sugar to a cream over a hot bain-marie. Gradually stir the hot vanilla milk into the creamy egg mixture, a little at a time. Squeeze the water out of the gelatine and dissolve in the hot cream, stirring constantly.

3 Chill the cream for approx. 30 minutes until it is just beginning to set. (To test: run the knife briefly through the cream. If it leaves behind a trail, it has reached the right consistency.) Whisk the double cream until stiff, then spoon into the setting vanilla cream mixture.

4 Transfer the cream into ramekin dishes, rinsed in cold water, and chill in the fridge until completely set for at least 4 hours or, ideally, overnight. Apricot purée makes a delicious accompaniment to this dessert.

Papaya cream
with cassis

Serves 4

2 papayas

8 large scoops vanilla ice
cream

8 tbsp cassis liqueur or
non-alcoholic cassis
syrup

lemon balm, to garnish

Preparation time: 10 minutes
(plus chilling time)
Per portion: approx.
164 kcal/689 kJ
2 g P, 1 g F, 31 g CH

1 Wash and peel the papayas, then remove the stones. Roughly chop the fruit, then place in a freezer bag and leave in the freezer for 20 minutes.

2 Place the chilled fruit and ice cream in a blender, and blend for approx. 1 minute. Transfer the mixture into four glasses or bowls. Swirl the liqueur or syrup over the surface in a circular motion, decorate with a sprig of lemon balm and serve immediately.

Tip: make sure that the papayas for this dessert are fully ripe or at least have yellow marks or stripes on the skin. Papayas which are completely green will not ripen. Ripe fruit can be identified by its colour (yellowish) and by gently pressing the flesh: the riper the papaya, the softer the flesh.

Sparkling wine mousse
with pomegranate kernels

Serves 4

6 leaves white gelatine
4 fresh eggs
75 g sugar
200 ml sparkling wine
1 tbsp lemon juice
150 ml cream
1 pomegranate

Preparation time: 35 minutes
(plus chilling time)
Per portion approx.
360 kcal/1512 kJ
11 g P, 19 g F, 24 g CH

1 Soften the gelatine in cold water, according to the instructions on the packet. Separate the eggs and chill the egg whites. Using a hand mixer, whisk the egg yolks and sugar together for 8–10 minutes until the mixture turns creamy. Stir in the sparkling wine (reserving 3 tablespoons) and lemon juice, a little at a time.

2 Squeeze the water from the gelatine, then place in a small saucepan with the remaining sparkling wine and heat over a very low heat stirring constantly, until the gelatine dissolves. Remove the saucepan from the heat. Begin by stirring 2–3 tablespoons of the wine-and-cream mixture into the gelatine, then fold this gelatine-and-cream mixture into the rest of the cream. Chill for approx. 30 minutes until the creamy dessert begins to set.

3 Whisk the egg whites and cream separately until both are stiff. Fold the cream, then the egg whites into the setting cream mixture. Cover and chill for at least 2 hours.

4 Cut the pomegranate in half. Using a spoon, tap the outer shell of the pomegranate halves to loosen the kernels, which should then drop out easily. Spoon the cream into bowls, a little at a time. Just before serving, sprinkle pomegranate kernels over the top of the cream.

Nougat parfait
with flaked almonds

Serves 6

100 g flaked almonds

4 eggs

3 tbsp sugar

3 tbsp honey

100 g nougat (firm enough
to slice)

250 ml cream

6 edible, candied orchids,
for decoration (from an
Asian food store)

Preparation time: 30 minutes
(plus freezing time)
Per portion approx.
440 kcal/1848 kJ
11 g P, 31 g F, 26 g CH

1 Toast the almonds in a frying pan without fat. Separate the eggs. Whisk the egg yolks, sugar and honey together for 5–6 minutes in a hot bain-marie until the mixture turns creamy. Dice the nougat and melt in another hot bain-marie. Stir the melted, lukewarm nougat into the egg mixture, then set aside to cool.

2 Line a loaf tin (approx. 1 litre) with foil. Beat the egg whites and cream together until stiff. First mix the almonds, reserving 1 tablespoon, into the egg mixture, then fold in the cream and, lastly, the stiff egg whites. Transfer the parfait mixture into the loaf tin, cover and chill in the freezer for at least 6 hours, ideally overnight.

3 Tip the parfait out of the tin and cut into slices or scoop out balls using an ice-cream scoop. Sprinkle with the remaining almond flakes and decorate each portion with 1 candied orchid before serving.

Poppy seed and marzipan quark
with cherries

Serves 6

4 tbsp milk
2 tbsp ground poppy seeds
1 sachet vanilla sugar
1 jar sour cherries (370 g)
½ vanilla pod
1 tbsp sugar
1 cinnamon stick
1 tbsp cornstarch
2–3 tbsp amarena cherries
  in syrup
75 g almond paste
500 g cream quark
100 ml cream
fresh mint, to decorate

Preparation time: 25 minutes
  (plus chilling time)
Per portion approx.
  330 kcal/1386 kJ
  12 g P, 20 g F, 18 g CH

1 Heat the milk, add the ground poppy seeds and 1 teaspoon of vanilla sugar, then bring to a boil and let the mixture stand for 10 minutes. Drain the cherries, reserving the juice (you will need 150 ml for this recipe). Slice open the vanilla pod lengthways and scoop out the pulp.

2 Bring 125 ml of cherry juice, the sugar, vanilla pulp, vanilla pod and cinnamon stick to a boil. Mix the cornstarch and a small amount of reserved cherry juice into a smooth paste, then add to the liquid in the saucepan. Simmer for 1 minute, then remove the cinnamon stick and vanilla pod. Take the saucepan off the heat and stir in the cherries. Leave the fruit mixture to cool before stirring in the amarena cherries.

3 Chop the almond paste, then purée with approx. 100 g quark. Stir in the rest of the quark, the poppy seed mixture and the rest of the vanilla sugar. Whisk the cream until stiff and fold into the poppy seed and quark mixture. Spoon alternating layers of poppy seed cream and cherry mixture into 6 dessert glasses, then decorate with mint leaves.

Panna cotta
with Marsala

Serves 6

4 leaves gelatine
250 ml cream
250 ml milk
pulp of 1 vanilla pod
3 tbsp sugar
½ tsp grated zest of
  1 unwaxed lemon
2 tbsp Marsala
peppermint leaves, to
  decorate

Preparation time: 20 minutes
  (plus cooking and chilling
  time)
Per portion approx.
  288 kcal/1210 kJ
5 g P, 21 g F, 21 g CH

1 Soften the gelatine in cold water according to the instructions on the packet. In a saucepan, bring the cream and milk to a boil with the vanilla pulp, sugar and lemon zest, and simmer for approx. 10 minutes. Thoroughly squeeze the water out of the gelatine, then dissolve in the milk mixture. Remove the saucepan from the heat.

2 Transfer the panna cotta into ramekin dishes, which have been rinsed in cold water, then chill for at least 6 hours until set. Tip out onto plates, drizzle with Marsala and decorate with mint leaves.

Info: literally translated, panna cotta means "cooked cream" in English. It is very simple to make and is one of the great classics of northern Italian cuisine.

Zabaglione
typically Italian

Serves 4

4 egg yolks

40 g sugar

100 ml Marsala

juice of ½ lemon

Preparation time: 20 minutes
Per portion approx.
  118 kcal/496 kJ
4 g P, 7 g F, 10 g CH

1 In a metal bowl, whisk the egg yolks and sugar together until frothy. Add 1 tablespoon of warm water and continue to whisk over a hot bain-marie.

2 Add the Marsala, then stir for approx. 10 minutes until rich and slightly thickened. Add lemon juice to taste.

3 Transfer the zabaglione to serving glasses and serve warm. Accompany with sponge biscuits or amarettini.

Tip: depending on the occasion or personal taste, the zabaglione can also be flavoured with cinnamon. In addition to Marsala, the traditional alcoholic ingredient, other alternatives include grappa, egg liqueur, Vin Santo, amaretto or other types of liqueur.

Gelato di espresso
with cocoa beans

Serves 4

12 egg yolks

200 g icing sugar

125 ml cold espresso

cocoa powder and cocoa
  beans, to decorate

Preparation time: 20 minutes
  (plus chilling time)
Per portion approx.
  443 kcal/1860 kJ
11 g P, 22 g F, 51 g CH

1 Whisk the egg yolks and icing sugar together in a hot bain-marie until thick and creamy. Stir in the espresso. Leave to cool for 30 minutes.

2 Place the mixture in a metal bowl, then leave to set in the fridge. Using a fork, whisk the ice cream from time to time to disperse the ice crystals. Sprinkle with cocoa powder and cocoa beans before serving.

Semifreddo al limone
with rum

Serves 4

250 ml mandarin juice
250 ml orange juice
250 ml grapefruit juice
125 ml lime juice
200 g sugar
100 ml rum
grated zest of 1 unwaxed
  orange

Preparation time: 20 minutes
  (plus freezing time)
Per portion approx.
  377 kcal/1583 kJ
1 g P, 1 g F, 72 g CH

1 Strain the freshly pressed juices through a filter, then blend with 250 ml of water. Add the sugar and rum, then mix thoroughly. Transfer to a metal bowl and place in the freezer for several hours.

2 Mix briskly with a fork or whisk from time to time. Serve garnished with orange zest.

Tip: for a creamier consistency, purée the mixture in the blender just before serving.

Index